MEN-AT-ARMS SERIES

EDITOR: MARTIN WINDROW

7⁹⁵

Foreign Volunteers of the Wehrmacht 1941-45

Text by CARLOS CABALLERO JURADO

Colour plates by KEVIN LYLES

OSPREY PUBLISHING LONDON

Published in 1983 by
Osprey Publishing Ltd
Member company of the George Philip Group
12–14 Long Acre, London WC2E 9LP
© Copyright 1983 Osprey Publishing Ltd

British Library Cataloguing in Publication Data

Jurado, Carlos Caballero
    Foreign Volunteers of the Wehrmacht 1941–45.
    (Men-at-Arms series; 147)
    1. Germany. *Wehrmacht*—History
    2. Arms and armour—Germany—History—20th
century
    I. Title   II. Series
    623.4′0943   U820.G3

    ISBN 0-85045-524-3

Filmset in Great Britain
Printed in Hong Kong

Acknowledgements
The author gratefully acknowledges the invaluable
assistance of Emilio Marin during preparation of
the colour plates references. He would also like to
thank Angel Navarro and German Ramos for their
help with translation; Alfredo Campello, and David
List.

This book is dedicated to Maribel.

Foreign Volunteers of the Wehrmacht 1941-45

Introduction

When one speaks of the units of foreign volunteers integrated into the German forces during the Second World War, one thinks automatically of the Waffen-SS: indeed, few military corps have been so international in composition as the Waffen-SS. But, in absolute numbers, more foreigners served with the other three branches of the Wehrmacht—army, navy, and air force—than in the Waffen-SS. This book deals with these latter services. For this reason we have excluded foreign SS units; formations and units with militia or paramilitary status formed for security tasks and not wholly integrated into the Wehrmacht; and the Spanish 'Blue Division'. These parallel subjects are covered in depth in MAA 34,

The Waffen-SS, MAA 142, *Partisan Warfare 1941–45*, and MAA 103, *Germany's Spanish Volunteers 1941–45*, which connect directly with many mentions in this text.

To determine the exact figures for foreign enlistment in the services covered in this book is almost impossible. Published figures for enlistments in the USSR—the largest group by far—vary remarkably, depending upon the author. During the war Soviet enlistment was estimated at a total of about 30 divisions; to this we must add, at least, three divisions of Croatians, about 50,000 Italian volunteers in the Luftwaffe, and Legions of

Oberfeldwebel Léon Degrelle (centre) with the commander of the Légion Wallonie, Hauptmann Lucien Lippert (right); the scene emphasises Degrelle's importance within the unit even when he was still officially an NCO. At left, the first pattern flag, in black with a red Burgundy cross.

An NCO of the Légion Wallonie is decorated with the Iron Cross 2nd Class—an ironic addition to a chest already covered with medals earned fighting Germany in the First World War.

volunteers from France and Belgium, so the total number must have been very considerable.

As to the reasons which induced so many tens of thousands to volunteer to wear the German uniform, we must conclude that anti-Communism was the most significant. This sentiment was common to Dutch sailors and Italian flak crews, to Cossack cavalry and Croatian pilots; and it is emphasised by the enormous increase in volunteers following the German invasion of Russia, from a basis of practically nothing before that date. All over Western Europe, 'Legions' of volunteers for the Eastern Front were formed. Eventually the Waffen-SS would absorb the personnel from 'Germanic' countries—Norway, Denmark, Holland, and the Flemish region of Belgium—while the Army took the remainder from France, Walloon Belgium and Croatia. And it was from this period, obviously, that the progressively larger flow of Soviet citizens to the German colours began.

Nationalism was another factor. The Croatians, for example, having achieved the independence of their region thanks to the German victory over Yugoslavia, knew that they would only be able to maintain a separate state if Germany won the war. Flemish nationalists aspired to a separation from Belgium as part of the re-arrangement of Europe which they hoped would follow a Germany victory. In the case of volunteers from colonial possessions such as India and Syria, the nationalist motive was obviously paramount.

Western European Volunteers

The 'Légion Wallonie'

The policy of the German occupiers of Belgium quickly leaned towards favouring one of the two great national groups—the Flemish. When Germany invaded the USSR many Belgians volunteered for 'the crusade against Bolshevism'. While Flemish volunteers were grouped into an SS Legion, the Walloons were accepted only by the Army.

Among the first to volunteer was Léon Degrelle, chief of the Walloon fascist 'Rexist' party. Due to his

political prominence he was offered a lieutenant's commission, but refused it, insisting on joining up as a private. Despite his lack of previous military experience he would earn several promotions in the field and many decorations; and, above all, he would become the spiritual 'motor' of this small unit, achieving a total ascendency over it. Because the majority of volunteers came from the Rexists the Legion did not suffer from internal political schisms, which bedevilled some other units.

With the official denomination of 373rd Infantry Battalion, the Legion, some 600 strong, was first attached to the 100th Jäger Division on the southern sector of the Russian Front. Its first great battle took place at Gramowaja-Balka during the Soviet counter-offensive of winter 1941, where 300 Belgians resisted greatly superior Soviet forces, suffering 30 per cent casualties but earning 35 Iron Crosses and the respect of their German comrades. The Legion crossed the Dniepr on 2 November and spent the winter in the Donetz Valley. In March 1942, having lost a third of its effectives and 20 out of 22 officers, it was withdrawn from the front. It fought again in May in the battle for Kharkov, and in July in the German general offensive, now

attached to the 97th Infantry Division. It advanced 800km in one month against minimal resistance, but when it arrived before the Soviet defensive lines in the Caucasus things changed. Fighting hard, the Legion reached Maikop and, in August, Tjerkakow; decimated once more, it was sent back to Germany to re-organise. By this time Degrelle was a lieutenant. The Waffen-SS, expanding fast and looking for likely sources of capable troops, had its eye on this unit which it had at first spurned. In June 1943, brought back to strength, the Legion officially became a Waffen-SS unit.

The only peculiarity of the Legion's regulation German Army uniforms was the armshield in Belgian colours bearing the legend 'Wallonie'. The soldiers were authorised to wear any First World War decorations to which they were entitled. The

The LVF's first commander, Oberst Labonne, displays the French-made pattern of French volunteer armshield, with a rounded lower edge and a white top strip.

first version of the Legion's flag was black with a red Burgundy cross; later the Legion flag, and the company flags, were in white with a red Burgundy cross and a silver armoured arm.

The 'Légion des Voluntaires Français'

At the same time as the Walloon Legion was being raised, France was contributing a 'Légion des Voluntaires Français contre le Bolshevisme', usually known as the LVF. The initiative came not from the Pétain government of Vichy, but from the fascist parties established in Paris, which for once forgot their internecine strife to form a combined organising committee. The most prominent French fascist leader, Jacques Doriot, joined the LVF as a sergeant-major. After training at Debica in Poland late in October 1941, the LVF was sent to Russia under the designation 368th Reinforced Infantry Regt. as part of the 7th Infantry Division. Composed of two battalions, it initially fielded 181 officers and 2,271 enlisted ranks; a third battalion passed through Debica only a month later. The first commander, whose brilliance was limited, was one Col. Labonne.

The LVF's baptism of fire in the Moscow sector coincided with the Zhukov counter-offensive of 1941–42. Decimated at Djukowa, the LVF lost virtually the whole of its 2nd Bn.; it was withdrawn from the front, and Labonne was removed. Thereafter the 1st Bn. (Maj. Lacroix) and 3rd Bn. (Maj. Demessine) were used exclusively for anti-partisan work behind Army Group Centre. It was only at the end of 1943 that a new 2nd Bn. went into the line, and shortly thereafter the three were grouped once again into a real regiment commanded by Col. Edgar Puaud. The LVF fought successfully against the partisans until, in summer 1944, it found itself in the path of the great Soviet offensive after the collapse of the German central front. At Bobr a *kampfgruppe* of some 300 legionaries defended themselves so stubbornly that the Soviet official dispatch spoke of 'two French divisions'. Withdrawn from the front, the surviving elements were re-grouped at Greifenberg in East Prussia. On 1 September 1944, over the objections of many of the surviving soldiers, the LVF was grouped with the French SS Volunteer Grenadier Regt. (formed in 1943, and also mauled in 1944) and Frenchmen from the Navy, NSKK, and Milice, into the SS Volunteer Assault Brigade 'Charlemagne', later to become, on paper, the 33rd SS Div. 'Charlemagne'. [This account corrects an error in MAA 34, which assumed a direct ancestry between the LVF and the SS Französisches Frw.Sturmbrigade. *Ed.*]

On the sleeves of the German uniform the French wore a national armshield, usually of German but in some cases of slightly differing French manufacture. Some also painted a tricolour flash on their helmets. In July 1942 the Vichy government instituted a 'Croix de Guerre Légionnaire' for award to French volunteers; of similar size and design to the conventional cross, this bronze decoration lacked the crossed swords, and had laurel foliage around the central medallion.

The LVF also had two successive models of flag. The first, a conventional square tricolour, bore yellow embroidery: 'Légion des Voluntaires' on the obverse, and 'Honneur et Patrie' on the reverse. This flag was donated by the Sponsoring Committee of the LVF, as the Vichy government only recognised the LVF as an 'entity of public utility' at this point. In 1943 the government presented a new flag, of the basic model used by French infantry regiments since 1879, with gold wreaths in each corner of the tricolour. The obverse bore gold embroidery: 'La France au 1ᵉʳRégiment de la Légion des Volontaires Français', and the reverse '1941–42 Djukowo' and '1942–43 Beresina'. Each battalion also had a flag.

The 'Phalange Africaine'

After the 'Torch' landings only Tunisia, of all France's North African territories, remained under Axis occupation and Vichy sovereignty. Feeling directly attacked by the Anglo-American landings, the Vichy regime attempted to raise a force of volunteers for service alongside the Italo-German army. Its formation was announced on 22 November 1942, under the odd title, 'Légion Impériale'; and the first unit—in the event, the only one—was born on 8 January 1943 as the 'Phalange Africaine', with a strength of 300 French and 150 Moslems. (This later declined to 200 Frenchmen.) After three months' training the Phalange was attached to the 754th Inf.Regt. of the German 334th Inf.Div. at the Tunisian front, seeing some

action and being re-named 'LVF en Tunisie' during the bare month which passed before the Axis surrender at the beginning of May.

The colonial uniform of the French Army was worn with the German helmet and DAK greatcoat.

Other Western European volunteers

Numbers of volunteers from 'Germanic' countries preferred to join the German Army rather than the Waffen-SS, but since they formed no national units their numbers are uncertain; a total of between 800 and 1,000 Dutchmen are known to have served, but other strengths are unknown.

In July 1944 one of the formations of pro-German security militia raised in Flanders, the 'Vlaamse Wacht', received German Army uniforms in place of their previous dark blue outfit, with standard rank insignia. At one time it was intended to use these four battalions, totalling 3,000 men, in defence of Flemish territory against the Allied

Officers of an LVF detachment leaving for Russia wear the standard German-made volunteer armshield, of more ornate shape and with a black top strip bearing the name 'France'.

advance; but in the event, most were sent to join the Flemish 27th SS-Div. 'Langemarck' on the Russian Front. Some personnel did see action during the Arnhem fighting, on the strength of several German *kampfgruppen*. While in German Army uniform they wore on the left forearm the same national shield patch as used by the Flemish Waffen-SS, although apparently this was often omitted as being too dangerous, in view of the special hatred felt by Belgian Resistance fighters for these collaborators.

The Kriegsmarine also recruited in Western Europe from July 1943 onwards. In broad figures, one may calculate that Holland supplied about 1,500 naval volunteers; Norway, about 500; and Flanders, about 300. They joined German crews individually or in small groups; and although in theory they could have worn national armshield patches, there is no pictorial evidence of this practice. In the case of Danish sailors there is evidence that some former members of the SS Freikorps Danmark retained the cuff-title on their naval uniform.

Walloon, French and Croatian volunteers, wearing armshields on different sleeves, attend a student congress.

The Luftwaffe also recruited in the occupied countries, the two main groups being Italians and Flemings. After the Badoglio armistice of 1943 many Italians chose to enlist in the Wehrmacht to carry on the war. There was an initial and unsuccessful attempt to raise a force entitled 'Aviazione Legionaria Italiana'. Later the new regime established by Mussolini as the Republica Sociale Italiana raised new armed forces, based upon Italian prisoners then held in Germany, at the same time as some 90,000 Italians were recruited into German formations. The most significant groups among these latter were the 50,000 or so who joined Luftwaffe flak units, and the 20,000 who joined the Waffen-SS. The flak volunteers served mainly in those units which were committed to the Italian front—the 4th, 19th, 20th and 25th Flak Divs. and 3rd, 18th and 22nd Flak Brigades. A certain number of former paratroopers of the 'Folgore' and 'Nembo' Divs. joined the Luftwaffe's 4th Paratroop Div., and Italians turned up in some technical units, e.g. two battalions of the 200th Luftwaffe Signals Regiment. As they did not form complete national units the Italian volunteers were governed by no regulation concerning national

Italian volunteers for the Luftwaffe flak branch wear standard Luftwaffe tropical uniform without national armshields. On the original print, however, one can make out the silver 'star of Savoy', traditional to Italian Army uniforms, worn on the tunic collars.

Balkan Volunteers

insignia; however, they often replaced some detail of their German uniforms with the Italian equivalent, such as the star of Savoy instead of the German collar patch.

A Flemish auxiliary security militia attached to the Luftwaffe, the four-battalion 'Vlaamse Fabriek Wacht' (from June 1943, 'Wacht Brigade'), was transformed into a flak unit after the Allied invasion of 1944. Their Luftwaffe uniforms do not seem, from available photographs, to have borne special national insignia, with the exception of some use of the Tollenaere Commemorative Badge—named after a Flemish SS-man killed at the siege of Leningrad. The so-called Flämisches Flak Brigade had a light anti-aircraft group of six batteries and a heavy group of four batteries. It saw no combat on Belgian soil, being moved into Holland, where some personnel saw action as ground troops at Arnhem. It later withdrew into Germany, fighting in the Rhine defences and finally in Bavaria.

In June 1941 the great majority of the countries of south-eastern Europe were allied to Germany: Rumania, Hungary, Bulgaria, Slovakia, and Croatia. All except Bulgaria sent contingents of their own forces to fight either on the Russian Front or as security troops in the Balkans. Croatia, as a newly independent state, could not send its own forces, but provided three Legions of volunteers.

The Croat Army Legion
Ten days after the opening of the campaign in Russia Ante Pavelic, the 'Poglavnik' (leader) of the Croat Independent State, called for volunteers to fight alongside Germany. The Legion was formed with three four-company infantry battalions, a staff company, an anti-tank company and a heavy weapons company. One battalion was raised entirely from Moslems in Bosnia-Herzegovina. Later an artillery group, with three batteries of 105mm guns, was added to the Legion, which in German Army parlance was designated 'Verstär-

Croatian volunteers of the 369th Div. swear allegiance to the Führer and the Poglavnik; note checkered shield decal on helmets.

(Top): Croat Air Force Legion badge, worn on right breast pocket, in silvered white metal with red/white checkers and black 'U'. (Left): Commemorative left breast pocket badge for survivors of Croatian 369th Regt wiped out at Stalingrad, in dull grey metal with red/white checkers. (Right): Croat Naval Legion badge, in silvered white metal with usual checkered shield. (Richard Hook)

ken Kroatischen Infanterie Regiment 369'—'369th Croatian Reinforced Infantry Regiment'. After training at Dollersheim it was attached to the 100th Jäger Div. on the southern sector of the Eastern Front.

The Legion fought effectively against partisans in the area of Poltawa, and in the advance towards Kharkov. It fought in the Stalino sector during the Russian winter counter-offensive of 1941–42, and in 1942 took part in the advance of the German 6th Army from Voronezh to Stalingrad; on 31 May 1942 an OKW communiqué congratulated the Croats on taking 5,000 prisoners, and in late July/early August they fought very hard at Kalatsch to force a passage of the Don. On 25 September the 100th Jäger Div. entered what would become its tomb: Stalingrad. The Croatians fought on a number of the hardest sectors of the perimeter during the agonising defence of the enclave, including the infamous Red October tractor factory. Very few of the Croat volunteers were evacuated, the remainder being killed or captured.

On German Army uniforms the Croats wore an

armshield of 25 red and white chequers beneath the legend 'Hrvatska' (Croatia). On all headgear they wore a gold oval badge with the letters 'NDH' (for 'Independent State of Croatia' in their own language) instead of the German eagle insignia.

The Croat Air Force Legion

This was composed of one fighter and one bomber squadron, equipped respectively with the Messerschmitt Bf109 and the Dornier Do17, and attached as extra Staffeln to Luftwaffe formations—'15.(Kroatische)/JG 52' and '15.(Kroatische)/KG 53'. They saw action over many sectors, the bombers raiding Moscow at one point, and the fighters reaching the Caucasus. The first Croatian volunteer to win the Iron Cross 1st Class was a fighter pilot, Lt. Mirosevic, the leading ace of the Air Legion with 46 victories. In mid-1944 the Croatian airmen returned to their own country to help fight off the partisan threat, which had by then escalated into full-scale war.

The Croatian airmen wore Luftwaffe uniform, insignia and decorations, with the addition of a winged national shield badge worn either in metal on the right breast pocket, or in cloth on the right sleeve.

The Croat Naval Legion

Mussolini, who wished to keep Italian dominance of the Adriatic Sea unchallenged, and who had established a 'protectorate' over the Croatian Adriatic coast, was opposed to the formation of a Croatian navy. The Croat Naval Legion thus went to the front without vessels of any kind. About 1,000 volunteers joined this unit, but they were obliged to appropriate some 60 light vessels—mostly fishing boats of between ten and 20 tons—abandoned by the Soviets. This makeshift flotilla, badly equipped and even worse armed, carried out coastal security duties in the Black Sea and Sea of Asov, facing much heavier and more formidable Soviet elements with some courage and resource. With the fall of Mussolini in 1943, and the ending of the Italian protectorate, Croatia formed a small navy with confiscated Italian vessels. Some small German vessels also operated in the Adriatic with mixed crews, or entirely Croatian crews sailing under the German flag. The seamen wore German uniform with the usual national armshield.

The German-Croatian Divisions

The annihilation of the 369th Inf.Regt. at Stalingrad was followed by the creation of new units to continue its tradition. On 13 March 1943 Pavelic announced the raising of a volunteer division which would carry the number '369'. Although the rank and file were almost entirely Croatian, many officers and NCOs were German, and it was commanded by the German Gen. Nicholdt. Comprising the 369th and 370th Inf.Regts. and the 369th Arty.Regt., it was at first destined for Russia; but the increasingly urgent need for reinforcements to fight Tito's partisans led to its commitment to combat in Yugoslavia. In late 1943 it was decided to raise a second division, the 373rd, comprising the 383rd and 384th Inf.Regts. and the 373rd Arty.Regt., and commanded by the German Gen.Zellner. A third Croatian division was created in 1944, numbered 392nd, comprising the 846th and 847th Inf.Regts. and the 392nd Arty.

Lieutenant pilots of the Croatian Air Force Legion. Below the Luftwaffe breast eagle is the Legion's winged badge, and above it a transitional pattern of the Croatian Air Force pilot's badge.

Regiment. Both these divisions were also deployed against Tito's partisans.

Personnel of these divisions wore the same German uniforms and Croatian cap and sleeve insignia as the old Army Legion.

The Eastern Volunteers

A few weeks after the opening of the Russian campaign one of the most surprising phenomena of the Second World War occurred: the enlistment of the first of hundreds of thousands of Soviet citizens as volunteers in the German forces. Ironically, due to Nazi racial preoccupations, the German High Command were completely opposed to the recruitment of Slavs. Nevertheless, it continued, and reached astonishing totals. We can never know the exact figures, but reputable authors have estimated that around 1½ million Soviet citizens served the Germans in some capacity—the equiva-

lent of three Army Groups. Many of these do not concern us here, because they enlisted either in Waffen-SS formations or in various local militia and police units. Even so, there were still two large groups which fall within our scope: the 'Hiwis', and the 'Osttruppen'.

Almost from the first day of the campaign individual Soviet deserters and prisoners offered their services for auxiliary duties; their total numbers can never be known, but these 'Hiwis', as they were generically called ('Hilfswillige', 'auxiliary volunteer') certainly represented several hundred thousand men. There were drivers, cooks, medical orderlies: any kind of 'dogsbody' who could free German troops for combat service—although the 'Hiwis' themselves naturally took up arms in emergencies. At first they retained Soviet uniforms stripped of insignia, and later received basic

Ante Pavelic, centre, with Croatian naval personnel on the Black Sea coast. The senior petty officer at bottom right displays the national armshield clearly, and it can just be made out on several other uniforms here. The officer on the Poglavnik's left wears the Croatian Medal of Bravery.

German uniforms; usually their only identifying insignia were brassards reading 'Im Dienst der Deutsche Wehrmacht'.

The second category, the 'Osttruppen' ('Eastern Troops'), includes all personnel integrated in formed units into the German forces; they were normally grouped in battalions termed 'Ostbataillonen'.

The first units were organised on a basis of 'private enterprise' by German unit commanders, in defiance of official orders. The bulk of them were recruited from non-Russian nationalities of the USSR—Balts, Ukrainians, Caucasians, Cossacks, etc. (It is important to remember that however monolithic the Soviet Union appears to the Western observer, it is in fact an empire of many different ethnic groups dominated by the 'Great Russians' of the heartland; and that even today, and certainly in the 1940s, many of these minorities felt themselves to be defeated and occupied nations ruled by foreigners. A Muscovite has no more in common, ethnically and historically, with a Caucasian than a Pole has with a Spaniard.)

The mission of these auxiliaries was mainly rear-area security. In November 1941 Army Group Centre organised the first six battalions, using the term 'Osttruppen'; and shortly afterwards German High Command authorised further formations, but with a number of restrictions. Two of these were that no battalion should muster more than 200 men, and that they should be employed solely as security guards. Shortly afterwards some police battalions recruited in the Baltic states would be sent to cover thin sectors on the northern part of the front, however. At the end of 1941 an order created several Legions of Asiatics and Caucasians, the 'Ostlegionen', whose status was at first considered identical to that of the European volunteer Legions.

In summer 1942 the Osttruppen were considered sufficiently important for an attempt to be made to regulate their chaotic uniform and insignia practices. It must be stated at once that this never succeeded, and that only representative practices can be described. The reasons for this are obvious. These units never served together in organised formations, but were scattered all over Russia. They drew personnel from many sources, and clothing reflected this extraordinary diversity. Some wore uniforms of German origin, often obsolete; others wore Soviet clothing, sometimes dyed; some wore 'official' insignia, others mixtures of official and German insignia, and yet others, elements of Tsarist styles. The 'freelance' manner in which some units were raised by parent German units led to logistic chaos, and the use of unauthorised insignia.

Three systems of collar patches were planned. One was to be for Russians and Ukrainians, one for the Asiatic and Caucasian Ostlegionen, and one for Cossacks. There were two sequences of shoulder straps, one for Russians, Ukrainians and Cossacks and one for Ostlegionen. All these designs, and standard German insignia, were used promiscuously by whoever received them, often mixed on the one uniform.

An armshield and a cockade in national colours were designed for each nationality. According to German ideas the Eastern volunteers were not entitled to wear the Hoheitsabzeichen—the German eagle and swastika breast badge—as this was a strictly German national honour. An alternative breast badge was designed featuring a diamond enclosing a swastika and supported by two stylised wings, in grey on field grey backing. This was seldom issued in practice, and the German eagle, or no breast badge at all, were more often seen.

An Eastern Peoples' Decoration for Bravery and

Gen.Andrei Vlasov addressing the first meeting of the KONR in Prague in December 1944. He wears his special personal uniform, of a light grey shade piped with gold and without insignia. In the foreground are Gens. Chilenkov and Malychkin. Note that, unusually, the ROA armshield is worn here on the right sleeve.

The first nationalities of Soviet volunteers to be accepted into the Wehrmacht in organised units were the Legions recruited from Caucasian and Asiatic peoples. This sergeant-major and second lieutenant of the Georgian Legion display the white-braided red collar patches authorised for these Ostlegionen; the Georgian armshield in red with black and white details; and the narrow shoulder straps authorised for native officers. The NCO displays the ribbon of the Eastern Peoples' Decoration 2nd Class in Silver, sewn into his buttonhole in German fashion. The Georgian Legion sent more than a dozen battalions to the front: one, the 823rd Ostbataillon, even ended up in garrison on Guernsey.

Merit, in five classes, was instituted in order to reward volunteers while denying them the honour of German decorations. In fact many German decorations were awarded, and in 1944 their use was officially authorised.

The Inspectorate of Eastern Troops was established on 15 December 1942, to supervise all these proliferating units; it was entrusted to Gen. Hellmich, succeeded in January 1944 by Gen. Kostring, and on the latter date it was redesignated as the Inspectorate of Volunteer Troops. The Inspectorate organised the training of new units, usually infantry battalions but also cavalry squadrons, engineer battalions and artillery

groups. But the Inspectorate did not have tactical command of the units in battle; each was subordinated to a German unit, either in the front line or in the rear areas. Each headquarters of a German Army or Army Group in Russia included a headquarters staff for Eastern troops. A military academy for training Eastern officers was set up at Mariumpol in Lithuania.

Far more than this Inspectorate, the driving force behind these units was an outstanding man whose personal charisma energised the gigantic movements of volunteers: the former Soviet general Andrei A. Vlasov. A distinguished commander in the defence of Kiev and Moscow, Vlasov convinced his German captors that he was willing to collaborate with them in order to bring down the regime of Stalin—as, indeed, were many other senior Soviet officers. Thanks to the support of some elements within the German Army Vlasov was able to create a committee, which in December 1942 published the so-called 'Smolensk Manifesto'; this formulated, for the first time, the desires of many hundreds of thousands of former Red Army men to

fight alongside the Germans to rid their country of Communist dictatorship.

At the beginning of 1943 the name 'Russkaia Osvoditelnaia Armiia' (Russian Liberation Army, abbreviated to 'ROA') began to be used to designate all battalions and companies of Eastern volunteers. However, it must be emphasised that this dispersed mass of units never constituted an Army in an organisational sense, despite the creation at Dabendorf of a kind of 'ghost' headquarters including seven Soviet generals and some 70 colonels; this HQ never in fact enjoyed any practical jurisdiction over the Ostbataillonen.

Opposition to the ROA and Vlasov's plans for its unification came from two quarters. Certain German elements were fanatical in their distrust of all Slavs; and volunteer units of minority nationalities like the Ukrainians and Caucasians were fighting specifically to free their countries from Russian rule, and had no interest in any 'Russian' Liberation Army. The anti-Vlasov German faction pressed for the disbandment of the Ostbataillonen, using as a pretext reports of desertion from ROA,

Two warrant officers (left) and a private (centre) display the collar and shoulder insignia authorised for Caucasian and Asiatic volunteers in this photo of a tour by the Grand Mufti of Jerusalem. The blue, red and green armshield of the Azerbaijan Legion catches the light, obscuring the white crescent and star on its central red stripe.

and by early autumn 1943 had almost succeeded in this aim. They failed when the Inspectorate of Eastern Troops was able to show that there were at least 427,000 Eastern volunteers—equal to some 30 German divisions, and a force no sane man would disband, given the Wehrmacht's manpower shortage. Nevertheless, due to lingering fears of a betrayal *en masse*, it was decided to send these volunteers to the occupied countries of Western and Southern Europe.

At the beginning of 1944 72 Eastern battalions were already in the West, and the Mariumpol academy was transferred to Conflans in France. (The only British territory occupied by Germany, the Channel Islands, received its share of these uprooted units: the Georgian 823rd Ostbataillon was posted to Guernsey, and the 643rd—which was actually Ukrainian, despite its ROA armshield—to

1st Lt. Dudanginsky of the Azerbaijan Legion displays the white-framed red collar patches of this rank, and the narrow Ostlegionen officers' shoulder straps. Again, the ribbon is that of the Eastern Peoples' Decoration 2nd Class in Silver.

A warrant officer wearing regulation rank insignia and, on the right sleeve, the armshield of the original 'Bergkaukasien Legion' which was later divided into the 'Nordkaukasien' and 'Aserbeidschan' Legionen: three yellow 'Cerberus' heads in 'wheel' arrangement on a blue background.

Jersey.) Since these troops had enlisted specifically to fight the Communist regime, their transfer to the West dealt a severe blow to morale. It is hardly surprising that there were some instances of mutiny, or that those units which found themselves in the path of the Anglo-American invasion did not fight with enthusiasm.

Vlasov never did overcome the suspicions of the non-Russian volunteers. The Asiatics and Caucasians were clearly opposed to his dreams for the ROA; and the Ukrainians even began to use the term 'Ukrainske Vyzvolne Viysko' (Ukrainian Liberation Army, or 'UVV') as a notional collective title for all the scattered Ukrainian battalions and companies. (Lacking a leading figure with Vlasov's energy and character, the UVV remained a name only.) When on 14 November 1944 Vlasov founded the 'Komitat Osvobozhniia Narodov Rosso' (Liberation Committee of the Russian People, 'KONR') only one ethnic group apart from the Russians joined it: the Kalmucks.

To detail such a vast number of small and dispersed units is impossible. It was only at the very end of the war that some Eastern Volunteer Divisions were incorporated. We do not even possess a reliable list of Ostbataillonen. According to a possibly incomplete German list of June 1943 there were already 68 battalions, one regiment and 122 companies at that date. An American list of 1945 lists 180 Ostbataillonen and three Ostregimente, but omits the divisions which are known to have existed then. For our purposes here we divide the units according to nationalities, or groups of nationalities; this has the merit of reflecting the different policies adopted by the Germans towards different ethnic groups, which sometimes affected organisation. An obvious example is that the first Cossack division was already formed in 1943, while the first Russian division did not exist until 1945.

Apart from the German Army, the Kriegsmarine and Luftwaffe also recruited in the East. We know practically nothing of the naval volunteers; but in the case of the Luftwaffe, totals of up to 300,000 men recruited in the USSR are mentioned, with an Inspectorate of Ostflieger commanded by Gen. Aschenbrenner. These men served mainly on ground duties at German airfields, but by the end of the war some 50,000 were serving in flak units; the few small flying units are dealt with separately, below.

The Ostlegionen

The first volunteers to become regular members of the German Army came from the Asiatic and Caucasian peoples of the USSR. Their territories lay beyond that part of the Soviet Union which Germany intended to occupy permanently, and encouragement of their nationalistic feelings thus presented no conflict of interest. Incorporated by force into the Russian empire only a few generations previously, they still had strong nationalistic feelings to encourage. Moslems and Orthodox Christians alike had strong religious reasons for opposing Communism. Finally, their ostensible 'liberation' by Germany might encourage other colonial peoples of Asia and the Middle East to identify Germany as a potential ally against British colonial power.

Numerous ethnic groups live in the Caucasus and in Soviet Central Asia, but the Germans sought to assemble them under two names only: the 'Caucasians', who lived on both sides of that mountain range, and the 'Turkomans', which name was to embrace all Asiatic tribes from the Volga to the remotest heart of the Asian steppes. When, in November 1941, the 444th German Security Division ('Sicherungsdivision') enlisted the first of these volunteers, they were grouped into a 'Turkoman Batallion 444' and a 'Caucasian Batallion 444'.

On 30 December OKW ordered the formation of

Gen. Hellmich, Inspector-General of Eastern Troops, visits a unit of the Turkestan Legion during training. The Asiatic volunteer appears to be wearing the German Army tropical uniform with standard blue/grey-on-tan collar and breast insignia, and German cap insignia.

several volunteer Legions from these nationalities, which were raised by the Army during the first half of 1942; at first four, and later six Legions were fully integrated, enjoying the same status as the European Legions, and at first based in Poland. The *Turkestan Legion* included Kazaks, Kirghiz, Uzbeks, Turkomans, Karakalpaks, and other minor tribes, and was stationed at Legionowo. The *Moslem-Caucasian Legion* (later renamed *Azerbaijan Legion*) was stationed at Jeldnia. The *North Caucasian Legion*, with men from some 30 different tribes from the northern slopes of the range, was at Wesola. The *Georgian Legion* was at Kruszyna, the *Armenian Legion* at Pulawy, and the *Volga Tartar Legion* at Jeldnia. A school at Legionowo trained NCOs (termed 'Gruppenführer' in these Legions) and officers ('Zugführer' and 'Kompanieführer' identifying lieutenant and captain respectively), under a German staff designated 'Kommando der Ostlegionen in Polen'.

In line with established policy these Legions were never grouped in the field; as soon as each battalion finished its training in Poland it was sent to the front line separately. The first unit to become operational was the 450th, drawn from the Turkestan Legion, and commanded by Maj. Mayer-Mader, former commander of the 444th Turkoman Bn. (see above). The 450th, and the 452nd, also from the Turkestan Legion, left Poland in spring 1942. In autumn 1942 a further wave of units was sent to the front: Ostbataillone 781–784 (Turkestan Legion); 795 and 796 (Georgian Legion); 800–802 (North Caucasian Legion); 804 and 805 (Azerbaijan Legion); and 808 and 809 (Armenian Legion).

The second wave left the training areas in spring 1943: Ostbataillone 785–789 (Turkestan Legion); 797–799 and 822 (Georgian Legion); 803 (North Caucasian Legion); 806, 807, 817, 818 (Azerbaijan Legion); 810–813 (Armenian Legion); and 825–827 (Volga Tartar Legion).

A third wave left for the front in the second half of 1943: Ostbataillone 790–792 (Turkestan Legion); 814–816 (Armenian Legion); 819 and 820 (Azer-

Typical Cossack unit of the Wehrmacht, showing a diversity of caps and uniforms, though all carry the traditional *shashka* **sabre.**

baijan Legion); 823 and 824 (Georgian Legion); 828–831 (Volga Tartar Legion); and 835–837 (North Caucasian Legion).

At the end of 1943 the Kommando der Ostlegionen in Polen was dissolved, having formed 14 Turkestani, eight Azerbaijani, seven North Caucasian, eight Georgian, nine Armenian, and seven Volga Tartar battalions: 53 in all, more than 50,000 men, who had been sent initially to Russia and later to Western Europe. But Poland was not the only place where units of these nationalities were formed. After the winter fighting of 1941–42 the German 162nd Inf.Div., commanded by a well-known specialist on Central Asia, Gen. von Niedermayer, was withdrawn from the central sector of the Eastern Front. Von Niedermayer was ordered to turn his formation into a training centre for Ostlegionen, and dedicated himself to this task from May 1942 to May 1943, with his headquarters at the Ukrainian town of Mirgorod.

The majority of the battalions trained by the 162nd Div. did not receive numbers in the same sequence as those formed in Poland, but instead the number of a battalion of a German regiment to which they were posted. Until the beginning of 1943 they were sent only to regiments serving on the southern sector of the front; thereafter they were also sent to the central and northern sectors. The following list of battalions/regiments is broken down into the constituent Legions:

Turkestan Legion—I/29, I/94, I/295, I/370, I/371, I/389, I/44, I/305, I/100 Jäger, I/384, I/297, I/76

Azerbaijan Legion—I/4 Gebirgsjäger, I/73, I/97 Jäger, I/111, II/73, I/101 Jäger

North Caucasian Legion—the exception: Ost-bataillone 842, 843

Georgian Legion—I/1 Gebirgsjäger, II/4 Gebirgs-jäger, I/9, II/198

Armenian Legion—II/9, I/125, I/198

The following units were in the course of training when in May 1943 the 162nd Div. was once more transformed into a combat formation:

Turkestan Legion—I/71, I/79, I/129, I/375, I/113

Azerbaijani Legion—I/50

Georgian Legion—III/9, II/125

Armenian Legion—III/73.

The 162nd Div. kept the German training staff, and its soldiers were drawn from the former depot battalions of the Ostlegionen. This German-

These volunteers may not actually be Cossacks, but definitely wear the Cossack crossed-lances collar patches on their German greatcoats. Note standard German cap insignia.

Turkoman formation was named the 'Turkoman Division', and in accordance with the policy for deploying Eastern units away from the USSR it was sent first to Slovenia and later to Italy, for anti-partisan duties. It spent the rest of the war in Italy, only brushing against Allied regular troops on two occasions, briefly and unimpressively.

Another unit composed of volunteers from these nationalities was the 'Sonderverband Bergmann', with a strength of three battalions; this unit apparently enjoyed some success after being parachuted behind Soviet lines in the Caucasus.

Of much greater numerical importance were units formed for auxiliary tasks in the German rear areas. The 'Boller Brigade' stands out. Composed of four 'Verstärken Turks Arbeits Bataillone' (Reinforced Turkoman Labour Bns.) and one depot battalion, it totalled 20,000 men. There were also ten other auxiliary Ordnance Store, Supply,

Note Cossack collar patch, and the authorised but rarely-photographed breast badge which replaced the Hoheitsabzeichen for Eastern troops: a swastika in a diamond supported by stylised wings.

Construction and Depot Bns., totalling 10,000 men. Independent companies reached a total of 202 Ordnance Store, Supply, Construction Engineer, Railway Construction Engineer and Road Construction Engineer Companies, of which 111 were formed from Turkomans, 30 from Georgians, 22 from Armenians, 21 from Azerbaijanis, 15 from Volga Tartars and three from North Caucasians.

Taking all these types of unit, the number of volunteers to serve in the Eastern Legions must have totalled at least 175,000. Each Ostlegion was supported by a national committee formed by eminent nationalist leaders and recognised by the Germans. Towards the end of the war, when Vlasov's KONR was becoming increasingly prominent, there was some agitation by these national committees for a consolidated Caucasian Liberation Army and National Turkestan Army, in order to defend their respective autonomies; but this talk came to nothing.

The Germans had foreseen the issue of special collar patches and shoulder straps to the Ostlegionen. In a special issue of the propaganda magazine *Signal* devoted to the Eastern volunteers there appeared illustrations of insignia which did not, in fact, see use. The *Signal* illustrations showed black collar patches with a system of white and silver bars and gold 'pips' identifying rank, and a thin edging in a different colour for each Legion. The patches of general officers bore national heraldic insignia on variously coloured national backings. An equally complex series of black shoulder straps had different coloured outer piping for each Legion, with NCO ranks identified by white transverse bars, and junior officers by broad silver chevrons and gold 'pips'. Field ranks bore even more complicated insignia.

In practice, this system was never used. Since native officers rarely rose above first lieutenant, and practically all company commanders were German, insignia for ranks from captain upwards were superfluous. The different coloured pipings were not used. In practice the patches were red, with a system of bars and pips. Officers' shoulder straps were simplified; they were similar, though not identical, to those of German 'Sonderführer' officials, symbolising German reluctance to accord these native officers the status of German officer rank.

The cockades and armshields which were worn by these Legions are illustrated in the colour plates and in the accompanying line and tone diagram. There were other examples of armshields apart from those illustrated in detail. The original Bergkaukasien Legion, later split into the Azerbaijan and North Caucasian Legions whose patches are illustrated, had a blue background bearing in yellow three equally spaced dog's-heads joined at the neck to a central circle, all facing to the left; this was the mythical Cerberus symbol. A first model of the Turkestan Legion patch was shield-shaped, with 'Turkistan' on the black upper strip; the shield proper was halved horizontally red over blue, with superimposed on the centre an arch and a horizontal arrow. The Volga Tartar Legion also used a variant of that in the line illustration: a blue-grey oval with a yellow border, it had an arch and a vertical arrow in the centre, with yellow lettering 'Idel-Ural' above and 'Tartar Legion' below. The round cap cockades were in the same combinations of colours as the armshields.

The Kalmucks

Although not included among the Ostlegionen, the Kalmucks were an Asiatic race of the USSR and should logically be dealt with here.

The first Kalmuck units were organised by the German 16th Mot.Div. after it occupied the Kalmuck capital of Elista during the 1942 summer offensive. They were known variously as the Kalmuck Legion, 'Kalmucken Verband Dr. Doll' (after the German organising officer), and Kalmuck Cavalry Corps. The status of this unit was different from that of the Ostlegionen; it was practically a 'free corps', with allied status and wide autonomy, and was largely composed of ex-Red Army men serving under native NCOs and officers, with only a small German liaison team. The Kalmucks were therefore not numbered in the Ostbataillonen sequence.

The strength of the Kalmuck Cavalry Corps continued to increase even when the Germans retreated from the Kalmuch Steppe. On 31 August 1943 it comprised: I Group (1st, 4th, 7th, 8th, 18th Sqns.); II Group (5th, 6th, 12th, 20th, 23rd Sqns.); III Group (3rd, 14th, 17th, 21st, 25th Sqns.); IV Group (2nd, 13th, 19th, 22nd, 24th Sqns.). The 9th, 10th, 11th, 15th and 16th Sqns. had been left behind Soviet lines in their homeland to carry out guerilla operations.

The Kalmucks fought initially against Communist partisans in their homeland, later retreating westwards with the German forces; again, they were used essentially for anti-partisan activity and for patrolling the coasts, and were only used in the front line in emergencies. They were successively attached to a number of German Security Divisions. Continuous retreats eventually brought them to Poland; and at the end of 1944 they numbered some 5,000 men. The Russian winter offensive of 1944–45 found them near Radom, and at the end of the war they were being re-organised at Neuhammer. The Kalmucks were, as mentioned already, the only non-Russian Eastern volunteers to join Vlasov's KONR.

In spite of their special status, their uniform was never determined. They seem to have worn cast-off German uniform mixed with items of national dress such as fur caps. It is not known if they received national armshields or cockades of their own.

The Cossacks

Although not initially accorded the privileged group treatment enjoyed by the Asiatic nationalities, those Cossacks who did enlist in the Legions officially recognised as part of the German Army soon attracted German attention as the most militarily skilled and loyal of the volunteers.

In August 1941 an entire Cossack regiment of the Red Army, led by its officers, deserted to the Germans. Under the command of Maj. Kononow, this unit was first designated 'Kosacken Abteilung 102', then 'Ost.Kos.Abt.600' in the Ostbataillonen sequence, and finally as the 5th Don Cossack Regiment. Many other small Cossack units were organised semi-officially by German units and local military authorities; before the end of 1941 Security Divisions had been authorised to raise Cossack squadrons or *sotnias*, and further recruitment was personally authorised by Hitler in April 1942. By this time many German mobile formations had raised their own Cossack auxiliaries, and there was significant Cossack recruitment by German cavalry units operating in the anti-partisan role in the rear areas of Army Groups. The most important and

A curious mixture of German and Tsarist Russian uniform is seen in this view of the blessing ceremony for a Don Cossack colour. The blue peaked cap with red band and piping, and blue breeches with a red side stripe, recall the traditional Don Cossack costume. The tunics appear to be German, with some examples of the Cossack collar patch.

only autonomous major unit, that of Kononow, achieved good results against partisans in Byelorussia. It is hardly surprising, then, that the idea of assembling squadrons into regiments and larger formations gained ground.

The first regiment, known as Regt. Von Jungschultz, went into action in the Atschikulak region in summer 1942, with satisfactory results. In September a German Cavalry officer, Gen. von Pannwitz, toured Cossack regions to test the feasibility of forming a complete Cossack division. Appointed Commander of Cossack Units, his first task was to organise the evacuation of many Cossack families who were fleeing the advancing Red Army, and to emplant a *stan* or Cossack settlement, first in Poland and later in northern Italy.

During March and April 1943, Von Pannwitz managed to concentrate several large Cossack

A Don Cossack, identified by his red and blue quartered armshield, wears Osttruppen shoulder straps but German Army collar patches and breast eagle.

units: the Von Jungschultz and Lehman Regts. from Army Group South, and the Kononow and Wolff Regts. from Army Group Centre. Transferred to the Mielau (Mlawa) training area in Poland, these units and smaller groups were reorganised into the 1st Cossack Div., of two brigades. The 1st Bde. comprised 1st Don, 4th Kuban, and 2nd Siberian Cossack Regts.; the 2nd Bde. comprised 3rd Kuban, 5th Don, and 6th Terek Cossack Regiments. In September 1943, in accordance with the new Osttruppen deployment policy, the 1st Cossack Div. was ordered to Yugoslavia to fight Tito's partisans. The high morale of the division, and the fact that the partisans were at least Communists, helped to compensate for the Cossacks' disappointment at being denied the chance to fight the Soviets. At the end of 1943, still in Yugoslavia, the two brigades were split and expanded into the 1st and 2nd Cossack Divs., which together with corps troops formed the 14th Cossack Corps.

The Cossacks fought long and hard against the partisans, and proved more successful in this kind of operation than the Germans; their horses gave them a useful tactical flexibility in the wild terrain of the Balkan mountains. When the Red Army advanced into Yugoslavia with its recent ally, the Bulgarian Army, the Cossacks had a chance to fight Soviet regular troops at last.

At the end of 1944 the corps was renamed 15th SS Cossack Cavalry Corps, but this was a 'paper' transformation only: officers and men were not looked upon as members of the Waffen-SS, and unit names and numbers remained unchanged. The corps—the largest formation within the Osttruppen—continued to grow. An un-numbered brigade of *plastum* or Cossack infantry, two regiments strong, was formed around the nucleus of the old 5th Don Cossack Regt., and, with the addition of various smaller units, formed a new 3rd Cossack Division. Shortly before the end of the war a Cossack infantry unit which had served on the Atlantic Wall, the 630th Inf.Regt., was also incorporated into the 3rd Div.; but it must be added that numerous other Cossack units continued to be scattered throughout the German Army.

Von Pannwitz greatly encouraged the use of traditional Cossack clothing among his volunteers; this was typical of the sympathy and understanding

which made him so popular among them, and which led to his being elected, before the end of the war, as *Feldataman*—the highest rank in the Cossack hierarchy, traditionally reserved for the Tsar alone.

Clothing included two types of fleece cap: the high *papasha* of Tsarist tradition, worn in black with a red cloth top patch by Don Cossacks, and in white with a yellow top by Siberian Cossacks; and the shorter *kubanka* introduced by the Soviets in 1936, worn in black with a red and a light blue top respectively by the Kuban and Terek Cossacks. All had a cross of silver or white braid on the top patch. Other headgear of German or Soviet origins was also worn.

Also retained were the *burka*, the heavy, stiff, square-shouldered riding cloak made from black camel or goat hair; the *baschlyk*, and the *tcherkesska*. The *baschlyk* was a deep hood with two long scarf-like ends, attached round the neck with a cord; the

Private and second lieutenant of Russian volunteers. The enlisted man wears a red-within-dark-blue oval cockade below the eagle on his sidecap, while the officer retains German insignia. Compare the private's plain black collar patch, with a white central stripe and silver button, with the officer's silver-edged version. The officer displays not only the officially-forbidden Hoheitsabzeichen, but also the Infantry Assault Badge; and the ribbons of the Eastern Peoples' Decoration 2nd Class in Bronze, together with that of the German Winter 1941/42 Medal—an unusual decoration for a 'Great Russian' volunteer, one would have thought.

tcherkesska, which could be worn at the same time, was the traditional heel-length coat decorated with *gaziri* (false 'cartridge' tubes) on the chest. Riding breeches, either in German field grey or traditional Cossack dark blue, retained whenever possible the stripes which identified the different Cossack nations: 5cm red stripes for Don, 2.5cm red stripes for Kuban, 5cm yellow stripes for Siberian, and 5cm black stripes edged with narrow blue piping for Terek Cossacks.

Cockades were at first round, bearing two crossed

Junior officers of Russian volunteers wear the ROA armshield in its regulation position on the left sleeve. Some wear enlisted men's belts; most display the red-within-dark-blue oval cap cockade alone, but at least one retains the German Army eagle.

white lances on a red ground—the design adopted for the collar patches of Cossack units. Later on large and small oval cockades, for officers and men respectively, were introduced in the colours of the different Cossack *voiskoi* or nations.

A variety of armshields was observed. The early models were of the same shape as those of other foreign Legions, and bore the names 'Terek', 'Kuban' and 'Don' on the upper black strip, above horizontal stripes in black, green and red (Terek); yellow, light blue and red (Don); and yellow and green (Kuban). Later patterns were simpler, and instead of names in Arabic letters bore only the two initials of the name of the *voiskoi*, in Cyrillic, above a shield diagonally quartered. The colours were as follows—top and bottom segments/side segments: Don, red/blue; Kuban, red/black; Terek, blue/black. The Siberian armshield was the last to appear; it had three Cyrillic initials above yellow/blue quartering.

These regulations, complex enough in themselves, were further confused in practice. Many Cossacks wore German headgear badges, sometimes including the death's-head if they served with Panzer formations. Collar patches could be standard German, Cossack, or of the patterns designated for Ostlegionen and for Russian volunteers; shoulder straps were equally mixed. There was no true standardisation, and the exotic was the norm—striped breeches, fleece and fur caps, traditional *shashka* sabres and *kindjal* daggers, all were used alongside modern German and Soviet uniform items and weapons. In two regiments—5th Don and 2nd Siberian—there were even medals awarded which were of regimental design.

The Baltic volunteers: Army

Although the best-known Baltic volunteer units served in the Waffen-SS, many soldiers from these countries served in both the German Army and the Luftwaffe.

Only weeks after the invasion of the USSR volunteers from newly-liberated Latvia and Estonia were recruited into indigenous police units. During

1: Private, Légion des Volontaires Français, 1942-43
2: Lieutenant, Phalange Africaine, 1943
3: Unteroffizier, Légion Wallonie, 1942

A

1: Hauptmann, Croatian Air Force Legion, 1942
2: Private, Croatian 369th Inf. Div., 1943
3: Petty officer, Croatian Naval Legion, 1942

B

1: Hauptmann, NSGr 12, 1944
2: Major, 658. Ostbataillon, 1943-44
3: Lt. Gen., Russian Liberation Army, 1944

1: Senior NCO, Don Cossacks, 1943
2: 1st Lt., Cossack Cavalry Corps, 1943
3: Trooper, Kuban Cossack, 1943

D

1: 2nd Lt. of an Ostbataillon, 1942-43
2: 2nd Lt., Terek Cossacks (?), 1944
3: Private, Russian Liberation Army, 1944

E

1: Senior NCO, Turkestan Legion, 1943
2: Major, German artillery, Osttruppen, 1944
3: 2nd Lt., Russian Liberation Army, 1944

1: 1st Lt., Armenian Legion, 1944
2: Warrant officer, Osttruppen, 1945
3: 1st Lt., Georgian Legion, 1944-45

G

1: Unteroffizier, Legion Freies Indien, 1944
2: Oberleutnant, Legion Freies Indien, 1944
3: Private, Legion Freies Arabien, 1943

H

the Zhukov offensive of winter 1941 some of these served in the front line; and thereafter many of these troops, having established a good reputation in combat, were absorbed into the German Army and issued with German uniform. With the creation early in 1943 of the Latvian and Estonian SS Legions, the Waffen-SS took over practically all Baltic volunteers, many of them veterans of Army units.

In autumn 1941 the German Army raised six Estonian Security Detachments, which were later transformed into three Ostbataillone (658, 659 and 660) and one Ostkompanie (657). The most famous of these units was the 658th Ostbataillon, led by Alfons Rebane, an Estonian who won the Knight's Cross before transferring to the Waffen-SS in summer 1944, taking command of a regiment of the Estonian 20th SS Division.

We can also identify some Latvian infantry battalions, and the Latvian 672nd Eastern Engineer Battalion, as well as many smaller units such as the 652nd Supply Co., and seven Construction Battalions.

In January 1944, with the German armies retreating along the Baltic coast, SS-Ogruf. Jeckeln suggested to OKW that autonomous governments be allowed to take nominal power in Latvia and Estonia, in order to mobilise the 1904 to 1923 draft categories as a basis for future national armies. This cynical idea was approved, and so-called 'Frontier Guards Regiments'—Grenzschutz-Regimenter—were raised, uniformed and armed by the Germans in February 1944.

The six Latvian regiments were sent to the front almost at once; poorly equipped and worse trained, they were so badly mauled around Dunaburg and Ostrow-Pleskau that they were progressively disbanded between July and September. Each regiment averaged 2,700 men; they were at first gathered in 'Kampfgruppe Jeckeln', but were later dispersed to German divisions: the 81st, 87th, 132nd and 215th Inf.Divs. and the 388th Field Training Division. After their disbandment the most serviceable survivors joined the '106th Waffen-Grenadier Regiment', subordinated to the Latvian 19th SS-Division.

The six Estonian regiments, totalling some 38,000 men, fared little better. Four of them, with German artillery and divisional troops and divisional staff from the disbanded 13th Luftwaffe Field Div., formed the 'Special Purpose Division 300' (Div.zbV 300), also known as the 'Estonian Frontier Guards Div.'; with a strength of 20,000 men this was the largest unit on the whole Narva front, and it was given the widest sector to cover. Divided into a 'North' (2nd and 4th Estonian Frontier Guards Regts.) and a 'South Brigade' (3rd and 6th Regts.), the division came under heavy attack on 18 September from the Soviet 2nd Assault Army. The division broke up as it fell back, isolated groups fighting among the marshes and mud-flats of Lake Peipus.

The only contribution by Lithuanian volunteers to the German Army was the formation of Construction Battalions. The personnel wore an armshield striped in yellow, green and red.

A Russian volunteer, just awarded the Eastern Peoples' Decoration 2nd Class in Bronze, wears neither Russian volunteer nor German insignia.

The Baltic volunteers: Luftwaffe

In June 1942 a unit known as See Aufklärungs Staffel 'Buschmann' began to recruit Estonian volunteers, and the following month it became the 15th Staffel of See Aufklärungs Gruppe 127. In time the whole Gruppe came to be Estonian; flying Arado seaplanes, they patrolled the Gulf of Finland. In October 1943, in a grim reflection of the changing fortunes of the Axis, the unit was transformed into Nacht Schlacht Gruppe 11: these 'Night Battle Groups' were ground-attack units equipped with the most obsolete of machines, on the grounds that the cover of darkness was a sufficient protection. The four Staffeln of NSGr.11 operated Heinkel He50s and even Fokker C-VEs on the Kurland front, particularly around Jöhvi, Rahkla, Reval and Libau. The unit was eventually disbanded for lack of fuel and spares in October 1944, but not before many personnel had escaped to neutral Sweden, crammed four to a plane into the ancient biplanes.

In March 1944 NSGr.12 was formed from Latvian volunteers, fielding three Staffeln by August; equipment included the Bucker Bu131, Arado Ar66 and Gotha Go145. The so-called Latvian Aviation Legion was completed by Flak-Abteilung 385, which served at Riga. The flying unit was disbanded in October 1944.

Apart from these units, some 6,000 Latvian and Estonian boys were recruited as Luftwaffen-Helfers, 'Air Force Auxiliaries', and sent to Germany. They served mainly in administrative and technical posts, but some were used by flak units. They wore Hitlerjugend uniform with nationally-coloured brassards.

Baltic volunteers, from both countries and in both main services, wore on German uniforms the same types of national armshield as their countrymen in the Waffen-SS, usually of German manufacture but sometimes of slightly different indigenous design. Details varied, but Latvian shields were generally red with a white diagonal

Gen. Vlasov, showing here the greatcoat and cap of his personal uniform, inspects an Ostbataillon; the man at extreme right wears a German 1916 helmet.

stripe across the centre, and Estonian shields were horizontally or diagonally striped in light blue, black and white.

The Russian volunteers

Although they were, of all peoples of the USSR, the least likely to be accepted as allies by the Germans, the Slavs of 'Great Russia' did fight in the German Army in considerable numbers. When the Ost-bataillonen were being formed, the following were regarded as ethnic Russian units, although numbers of Ukrainians and Byelorussians were probably to be found in their ranks: Ostbataillone 263, 308, 601–620, 627–650, 653, 661–666, and 674—a total of 54 battalions.

As Hitler's plans included the complete crushing of the Russian nation, it was extremely hard for the Germans to accept any show of nationalism within the Russian Osttruppen. The first example of this was the anti-partisan militia of the Orel-Kursk region which earned such a black reputation under the leadership of Bronislaw Kaminski. This rabble, of various nationalities called themselves the Russian National Liberation Army ('Russkaia Osvoboditelnaia Narodnaia Armiia', RONA) but were more widely known as the 'Kaminski Brigade', and were later designated the 29th SS-Division.

Another and more respectable experiment was carried out by Army Group Centre, who in 1942 enlisted a formation called the Russian People's National Army ('Russkaia Natsionalnaia Narod-naia Armiia', RNNA). The Germans also knew it by other titles, including 'Ostindorf Brigade' after the town where it was stationed, and 'Experimental Centre Unit', because it was an experimental project of Army Group Centre. It comprised six battalions, commanded by the former Soviet Gen. Boiarsky, and was unusual among Ost-truppen in that all ranks, including officers, were Russians. The uniform was basically that of the Red Army with insignia removed. In December 1942 the possibility of sending the brigade to the front was discussed, but because of German distrust of Russian personnel it was decided to break it up and send the battalions separately. This was a deep disappointment to those Russians who dreamed of a national force allied to the Reich.

As already described, the idea was taken up again

A Russian pilot of the KONR's small air element: note red-within-blue cockade of oval shape, with a silver outer edging, incorporated into the Luftwaffe officers' cap insignia. He appears to wear leutnant's collar patches but senior NCO shoulder straps.

by Gen. Vlasov. Despite the failure of the RNNA experiment, and despite the hostility of some elements both in Germany and among the non-Russian Soviet volunteers, Vlasov pressed ahead with his 'Smolensk Manifesto' and his programme of political-military propaganda. From 1943 onwards the name of the Russian Liberation Army, ROA, was heard with increasing frequency, and Vlasov emerged as its natural leader. At last, in October 1944, he was allowed to create a 'government in exile' in the form of the Committee for the Liberation of the Russian Peoples, KONR. On paper, the Germans gave permission for the formation of an army of five divisions, and practical attempts to achieve this began after KONR's first public appearance in Prague on 14 November 1944.

In fact, as already described, this army came to virtually nothing. The situation at the crumbling front did not allow the withdrawal and concentration of the dispersed Ostbataillonen, nor the transfer of the thousands of Russian slave workers who had been brought to work in German war industries. Recruits came from more recent Soviet deserters and PoWs, who naturally lacked the motivation of the earlier volunteers; and from the highly dubious personnel of the two recently disbanded Russian divisions of the Waffen-SS, the 29th and 30th, who were largely Kaminski's murderers, and Byelorussian 'security policemen', respectively.

From this unpromising background the first Russian divisions of the German Army emerged at last—when it was far too late to hope for any success in toppling Stalin, whose armies were hammering at the gates of the Reich. The divisions were named '600th Panzergrenadier Div.' and '650th Pan-

zergrenadier Div.', and were formed at the Munsingen and Heuberg training areas. A third division was in the process of formation at the end of the war; and some small units were also formed, including a depot brigade, a technical battalion and an officers' school.

The KONR also had its own tiny air element. By December 1943 the Luftwaffe had created the '1.Ostfliegerstaffel (russische)' (1st Eastern Squadron—Russian). This small unit operated a mixture of German machines of obsolete type and captured Soviet aircraft, until its disbandment in July 1944. The KONR air force, commanded by Gen. Maltsev, had a nominal strength of three squadrons (fighter, light bomber and reconnaissance), a flak regiment, a parachute battalion and a signal battalion. How far these achieved any physical reality is uncertain.

In January 1945 KONR had a total strength of around 50,000 men. On the 28th of that month it was officially declared that the Russian divisions no longer formed part of the German Army, but would be directly under the command of KONR. This empty gesture underlined the abandonment of

A group of Ukrainian volunteers, representing their unit, swear allegiance on the German war flag and their national flag—blue and yellow, with the black 'trident of Volodymyr' national emblem. The only visible insignia here are helmet-shields halved diagonally, blue over yellow.

these unhappy men, and it is not surprising that the under-equipped and poorly trained divisions now directed their animosity against the Germans. After several engagements in Silesia Gen. Buniacenko's demoralised 1st KONR Div. was to be found supporting the rising by non-Communist Czechs in Prague on 7 May 1945, in the hope of ingratiating themselves with the Allies. It was a vain hope.

The Russian volunteers wore their own collar patches, shoulder straps, cockades and armshields. The former are illustrated in the colour plates and diagram. The cockade was oval, blue outside red. There were at least three versions of the armshield. One was of the standard pattern for foreign armshields, with the word 'Russland' on the upper strip, and a blue double-armed Russian Orthodox cross on a white background. A simpler type substituted horizontal stripes of white, blue and red. The definitive type, on a broad field grey backing shield, had yellow Cyrillic initials on the top strip— 'ROA', which appears as the Arabic 'POA'. The white shield had a thin red edge and bore a blue St. Andrew's cross. The KONR also designed its own armshield, but this was only made privately and in insignificant numbers.

The Ukrainian volunteers

The only units of Eastern volunteers which formed part of the Wehrmacht at the beginning of the Russian campaign were two small Ukrainian battalions which had been created in spring 1941. The 'Nachtigall' Bn., recruited from Ukrainian minorities in Poland, is said to have worn German uniform with Ukrainian insignia. The 'Roland' Bn., raised from Ukrainian exiles living in Germany, is described as wearing its own uniforms patterned after those of the 'Western Ukrainian Army', an independence army which had fought the Poles from 1918 to 1920; no further details are known.

At the outset of the campaign both units, often wearing Soviet uniform, carried out commando-type operations. But internecine squabbling by different nationalist factions, and German resistance to any suggestion of Ukrainian autonomy, led to their disbandment in October 1941, although their strength totalled some thousands.

Ukrainians continued to collaborate with the Germans, however; a large number of volunteers

Although never used in Africa or the Mediterranean theatre, the Free Indian Legion were issued with tropical uniforms, including shorts.

came forward for local security and anti-partisan militias raised by the Germans in the occupied zone, and many others enlisted in the Ostbataillonen.

Once the idea of forming the ROA had been mooted, there was some discussion of forming a parallel Ukrainian Liberation Army ('Ukrainske Vyzvolne Viysko', UVV) incorporating the scattered units of Ukrainian volunteers, whose total number had been estimated at some 180,000. Unlike the ROA, the UVV lacked a charismatic and resourceful leader of Vlasov's calibre; what they shared was that both were armies only in name, lacking any practical authority over their notional units. Indeed, to a large extent the UVV was a propaganda tool of the German faction which wished to discredit Vlasov, born of their desire to fragment the recruiting drive among potential ROA personnel.

German uniforms were worn with an oval cockade, yellow outside light blue, and an armshield. Two patterns seem to have been worn. The earlier model was of standard design, with the legend 'Ukraine' above a shield of light blue bearing a yellow Ukrainian trident motif. The later type was halved yellow over blue and bore a white trident, with the legend 'UVV' ('YBB', to eyes accustomed to Arabic script) in white at the top.

Only at the very end of the war did the Ukrainian volunteers find an effective leader in Pavlo Shandruk, who had fought with the Ukrainian anti-Bolshevik nationalists years before, and who had later become a general in the Polish Army. Refusing to join Vlasov, he got permission to form the Ukrainian National Army, UNA, early in 1945.

Mixture of turbans and German field caps within a group of Free Indian Legion volunteers being trained on 20mm flak guns by a Luftwaffe NCO. The shade of olive-khaki evidently varied as widely among the tunics and caps used by this unit as among DAK troops.

Although operating under the same difficulties which prevented ROA and KONR forming a practical military force, Shandruk did manage to create two divisions in April 1945. The 1st Div. came from the surviving rump of the former 14th 'Galician' Div. of the Waffen-SS, formed two years earlier from Ukrainian minorities in Poland. The 2nd Div. was formed from some scattered German Army units, notably the 281st Ukrainian Reserve Inf.Regts., two guard regiments, and a Ukrainian anti-tank brigade. The UNA's total strength has been assessed at about 40,000. The 1st Div. saw some action in Austria and the 2nd in Czechoslovakia in the final weeks of the war.

As soon as the UNA was authorised Shandruk ordered new national insignia to replace German distinctions on the German uniforms. There is evidence that these were being worn on the former Waffen-SS uniform within the 1st Div. by the last weeks of the war, alongside new rank insignia, but it is unlikely that they were widespread.

Volunteers from the Russian Exile
During and following the Bolshevik Revolution many people had fled from the USSR. Many, making the most of the opportunity offered by the German invasion, returned to fight against the Communists. They enlisted in the Osttruppen—there were large numbers of exiles in the Cossack Cavalry Corps—or in Army or Waffen-SS units recruited in Western Europe. The most interesting case is that of the Russian Defence Corps in Serbia

('Russisches Schutzkorps Serbien', RSS), of which it has been said, with reason, that it was the last unit of the Russian Imperial Army. It was recruited among the large number of White Russians who had taken refuge in Serbia in 1921, and who had maintained their national identity and traditional loyalties. Their mobilisation to fight Tito's Communist partisans in the aftermath of the invasion of Russia was supported by the Germans; and at its peak the RSS, led initially by the White Russian Gen. Staifon and later by Col. Rogozine, reached more than 11,000 men in five regiments. At first the uniform was based on pre-war Yugoslav patterns, with one intriguing feature: former officers of the Imperial Army wore imitation Tsarist shoulder boards bearing their former rank insignia, whatever their rank in the RSS. Standard German uniforms were later supplied. (The early pattern of uniform is illustrated in a colour plate in MAA 142, *Partisan Warfare 1941–45*.)

The End for the Eastern Volunteers
Under the Yalta Agreements the Western Allies had promised to hand over to the USSR any Soviet collaborators who fell into their hands. This undertaking, perhaps felt reasonable enough at the time, led to a tragedy of enormous proportions when the war ended. All the major Eastern volunteer formations had attempted to surrender to the Western Allies; the Cossack Cavalry Corps had succeeded, as had the 162nd 'Turkoman' Div., the 1st Div. of the ROA, the bulk of the UNA and the RSS. (The fate of dozens of other Eastern battalions is impossible to determine, but easy to guess.)

Practically all the major units were handed back to the Soviets by the Western Allies, often amid the most heart-breaking scenes: it must be remembered that many of the Cossacks were accompanied by their women and children, and that none had any illusions about the fate that awaited them at Stalin's hands. The victims' pleas for mercy, and the representations made by Allied soldiers of all ranks who were sickened by their task, fell on completely deaf ears; only in the 1980s is this horrible episode being freely discussed in Britain. Hundreds of thousands of men, and large numbers of their families, disappeared into the appalling embrace of the NKVD. Nearly all the ringleaders of the volunteer movement were executed, beginning with Vlasov. Several senior German officers who had served with these troops—including Gen. von Pannwitz, who had refused to leave his Cossacks in their hour of peril—were hanged. Most officers, and many of their men, were executed; and the survivors were swallowed up by the *Gulag*, from which few ever returned.

There were only two major exceptions. The RSS nearly all held Yugoslav citizenship; and the 1st Div. of the UNA were able to argue that their former Polish status exempted them. (Ukrainians generally seem to have been among the luckiest survivors of these terrible years; a large group of former comrades of the 1st Div. soldiers, who had deserted *en masse* from the 14th SS-Div. on the Russian front and had remained together in hiding in rough country, actually fought their way through to safety in the American Zone of Germany as late as the winter of 1946–47.)

*   *   *

Non-European volunteers

For obvious reasons, the Germans could not recruit significant numbers of volunteers outside Europe and the USSR. Even so, they did create both Arab and Indian units, to use as propaganda in their programme of undermining the British and French Empires.

The Free Indian Legion

Some months before Operation '*Barbarossa*', while the German–Russian Non-Aggression Pact was still holding, the Indian extremist nationalist leader Subbas Chandra Bose arrived in Berlin from Moscow, intent on obtaining German help to free his country. Thanks to his zeal, he managed to persuade the Germans to recruit a volunteer group from among the many Indian troops of the British forces captured in North Africa. By the end of 1942 this 'Legion Freies Indien' had reached about 2,000 men, officially forming 'Indisches Inf.Regt. 950' of the German Army. This comprised three four-company battalions; companies of infantry guns (13th Co.), anti-tank guns (14th Co.), and Engineers (15th Co.); a fourth replacement-and-depot battalion; an Honour guard company (Ehrenwachkompanie); and a hospital/convalescent home. Partially motorised, the regi-

ment was later redesignated as a Panzergrenadier unit.

In 1943 Chandra Bose travelled to Japanese-occupied Singapore by submarine to help organise the parallel 'Indian National Army' recruited from Indian prisoners in Japanese hands, while the Free Indian Legion remained in Europe. It was stationed south of Bordeaux as part of the Atlantic Wall garrison. After D-Day it was withdrawn to Germany, and on 8 August 1944 came under the control of the Waffen-SS, enjoying a relationship similar to that of the Cossack Cavalry Corps. The unit never saw combat, and was eventually disbanded on Hitler's personal order.

The Legion wore the German Army's tropical uniform, Sikh personnel replacing the field cap with the turban. An armshield was worn high on the right sleeve: the legend 'Freies Indien' appeared in black on a white upper strip, above horizontal

The Free Arab Legion armshield is just visible at bottom left, in this photo of a volunteer in German tropical uniform. Turbans or tropical field caps were optional.

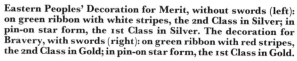

Eastern Peoples' Decoration for Merit, without swords (left): on green ribbon with white stripes, the 2nd Class in Silver; in pin-on star form, the 1st Class in Silver. The decoration for Bravery, with swords (right): on green ribbon with red stripes, the 2nd Class in Gold; in pin-on star form, the 1st Class in Gold.

stripes of orange, white and green, with a superimposed yellow and black tiger leaping diagonally towards the top right corner, the whole outlined black. The only other special feature of the uniform was a decoration instituted by the Committee for a Free India ('Centrale Freies Indien'), the political sponsors of the Legion. The Order of Azad Hind came in two categories and three classes, its design resembling that of the Eastern Peoples' decoration and its ribbon being striped vertically in national colours. The number of awards is unknown.

The Free Arab Legion

When the anti-British revolt led by Rashid el Galiani flared up in Iraq on 2 May 1941, the Germans formed a special staff, 'Sonderstab F', to channel help to the Arab insurgents. To support and exploit the revolt two small units were raised, 'Sonderverbande 287' and '288', drawn from personnel of the Brandenburg Division; but the revolt collapsed before they could be used in the field. Sonderverband 288, whose personnel were entirely German, was sent to operate with the Afrika Korps in North Africa. Sonderverband 287

remained in Greece, near Athens, and organised pro-Axis Arab personnel from the Middle East; these were mainly Palestinian followers of the pro-German Grand Mufti of Jerusalem, and Iraqis who had supported El Galiani. Eventually reaching a strength of three battalions, the unit was trained in Greece in tropical warfare. One battalion would eventually be sent to Tunisia, while the other two fought partisans first in the Caucasus and later in Yugoslavia. Sonderverband 287 was never officially designated as the 'Free Arab Legion', which latter was simply a generic name denoting those Arabs who fought under German command, differentiating them from certain other groups.

One of these was the 'North African Legion' formed from Moslems resident in France, and used as an anti-partisan militia. A significant number of these French-resident Moslems also enlisted in the LVF. An experiment was also carried out by the German 715th Inf.Div., in garrison in the south of France; this formation raised a unit of French-resident Moslems designated 'Deutsch-Arabische Inf.Btl.845'.

The largest Arab unit of the German Army was raised in Tunisia, and was variously known as the 'Deutsch-Arabische Lehr Abteilung' or simply 'Deutsch-Arabische Truppen'. The order of battle of 5th Panzer Army gives it a strength of five battalions, including a battalion absorbed from

Sonderverband 287, and the Moslem personnel who had originally enlisted in the Phalange Africaine—see above; there was also a good deal of local recruiting. Led by a cadre of Brandenburgers, it was used for rear area security.

Arab volunteers of these various units wore the German Army tropical uniform with an armshield high on the right sleeve. This had vertical stripes of green, white and black below a segment of red bearing two white stars, and black-on-white upper and lower stripes reading 'Freies Arabien' in Arabic and German respectively.

The Plates

A1: Private, Légion des Volontaires Français, 1942–43
Photos show both early and late qualities of German Army tunic in use by the LVF, with and without dark green badge-cloth collar and shoulder straps. The field service quality collar patches and white-piped shoulder straps are standard German infantry private's issue, as are all other items of uniform and equipment. The German-made national armshield is shown here; and a French tricolour shield has been painted on the helmet, right side only.

A2: Lieutenant, Phalange Africaine; Tunisia, 1943
A French colonial volunteer officer of the unit attached to the German 754th Inf.Regt. for the final weeks of fighting in Tunisia is shown wearing the characteristic combination of French and German uniform. The khaki four-pocket service tunic had a stand-and-fall collar with rather long points, worn buttoned to the neck with a khaki shirt and tie just visible above the edge; these details are obscured here by the *cheich*, the traditional desert scarf of French colonial troops. The combination of khaki tunic and pale twill breeches was common; a lighter colonial uniform made entirely of sand-coloured drill cloth was also used. The sand-painted DAK helmet has the rectangular tricolour flash used by the Phalange painted on the right side; and the only uniform insignia, apart from the first lieutenant's gold bars above the cuff, is the black and yellow patch of the Phalange on the right breast pocket. The double-bladed axe motif was widely used by the Vichy regime. The greatcoat is

The standard pattern of armshield for some Ostlegionen: 'Nordkaukasien'—green over red, white details; 'Aserbeidschan'—blue over red over green, white details; 'Armenien'—red over dark blue over orange, orange lettering; 'Georgien'—red, details black and white; 'Turkistan'—bluish green, white mosque, dark blue details on central dome, yellow secondary domes and crescents, dark blue lower lettering, yellow upper lettering; 'Idel-Ural' (Volga Tartar Legion)—dark blue over green, yellow edge and lettering, white central motif.

standard DAK issue; since it was made to have German shoulder straps of rank and branch added, it has no straps here.

A3: Unteroffizier, Légion Wallonie, 1942
This NCO wears absolutely standard German Army infantry uniform, with the silver *Tresse* of this rank at collar and shoulder straps. His tunic is of the superior early pattern, with dark green badge-cloth details. The Légion Wallonie wore the national armshield, of standard German-made pattern, on the left sleeve. This sergeant has been awarded the Iron Cross 2nd Class (ribbon in buttonhole) and the Infantry Assault Badge is pinned to his left pocket.

B1: Hauptmann, Croatian Air Force Legion, 1942
This volunteer fighter pilot of 15 (Croatian) Staffel, Jagdgeschwader 52 wears standard service dress for a Luftwaffe aircrew officer apart from the silver and enamel badge of the Air Force Legion pinned to his right breast pocket. Cap and collar piping and insignia are in the silver of commissioned ranks; the shoulder strap underlay and collar patches are in the yellow of flying personnel; and the rank is indicated by two gilt 'pips' on the former, and three silver embroidered 'wings' and an oakleaf spray on the latter. The gold and silver finish Pilot/Observer's Badge, the qualification insignia for a single-seat aircraft pilot, is pinned to the left breast pocket, and above the pocket is the bronze and black War Flight Clasp (*Frontflugspange*), this class being awarded for 20 missions. A photo in the body of the text shows Croatian pilots wearing no less than three winged badges on the right breast: the Luftwaffe's special *Hoheitsabzeichen* and the Air Force Legion badge, as here, and Croatian pilot's wings as well.

B2: Private, Croatian 369th Infantry Division; Balkans, 1943
An infantryman of the first Croatian-German division raised after the annihilation of the 369th Inf.Regt. at Stalingrad, this soldier wears standard German uniform of the period. The tunic is entirely field grey, and has unpleated pockets; the trousers are tucked into grey-green canvas anklet gaiters worn with laced ankle boots. A simple decal of the Croatian checkered shield insignia is applied to the right side of the helmet, and a more ornate national armshield, in the usual German-made pattern and bearing the legend 'Hrvatska', is worn on the left sleeve.

B3: Petty officer, Croatian Naval Legion; Black Sea, 1942
The regulation Kriegsmarine seaman's landing uniform is worn here, with the blue jumper tucked into the bell-bottom trousers, which are rolled at the ankle above marching boots. The 'boarding cap' and jumper bear German national insignia in yellow thread, and the rate badge on the left arm is also in yellow. Above it, the 'Hrvatska' armshield is of the same pattern as worn by the Army volunteers.

C1: Hauptmann, Nacht Schlacht Gruppe 12, spring 1944
This Latvian volunteer pilot, flying ancient Arados and Gothas on hazardous night ground-attack missions on the Narva front, wears the standard Luftwaffe officer's field service uniform of the period. The good-quality officer's version of the 1943 *Einheitsfeldmütze* has silver crown-seam piping and insignia. All normal insignia of rank and branch are worn on the fly-fronted *Fliegerbluse*, which for officers had slash side pockets. The field service shirt is pale blue. The Pilot/Observer's Badge is worn on the left breast, and above it the War Flight Clasp in silver, for 60 missions, with a black winged bomb replacing the fighter pilot's winged arrow in the central cartouche. The armshield is the only national peculiarity; there were several different Latvian patterns, all basically of this design but some bearing the legend 'Latvija' in white, either in the left corner or on a top strip.

C2: Major, 658.Ostbataillon, 1943–44
Based largely on photos of Alfons Rebane, the highly decorated Estonian Legion officer who commanded this unit before transferring to the Estonian 20.Waffen-Grenadier Division der SS. The high fighting reputation and special status of the Baltic units among the Ostbataillone are reflected in the impeccable German Army officer's service dress, differenced only by the national armshield in pale blue, black and white, with three yellow lions superimposed. (A simplified shield without the lions, and in two different shapes, was seen in 1944 on Army (right sleeve) and Waffen-SS (left sleeve) tunics. The cap and tunic bear standard German Army infantry major's ranking and piping. In addition, this officer has been awarded the Infantry Assault Badge (left breast), Iron Cross 2nd Class (ribbon), Iron Cross 1st Class (pin-on pattern, left breast) and Knight's Cross (worn on Ribbon at throat).

C3: Lieutenant-General, Russian Liberation Army, 1944
The uniform is basically that of a German Army general with ROA cap insignia, collar patches, shoulder boards and armshield. The gold-piped general's service cap has an oval cockade in red, blue and white metal. For this rank the black collar patches have gold piping, central stripe and button. The black shoulder boards are piped red and have a zigzag of gold lace, with a silver 'pip' denoting this particular rank. The ROA armshield on a field grey backing features a blue St. Andrew's cross on white, with the Cyrillic initials above—to Western eyes, 'POA'. The breeches have the red stripes and piping of a German general officer.

D1: Senior NCO, Don Cossacks, 1943
A typical combination of Russian and German uniform items—the Russian fleece *papasha* and soft leather boots worn with German M1936 tunic and trousers. The cap, which has a red top patch and silver lace cross, bears a German Army silver-grey metal eagle above a Russian cockade. German NCO *Tresse* encloses Cossack collar patches with

green enlisted ranks' edging. The shoulder straps have two white rank bars, worn close to the button. On the left sleeve is the second pattern armshield for the Don Cossacks, in red and blue. Like many Osttruppen this NCO is armed with the Soviet PPSh.41 sub-machine gun, and carries ammunition in a Red Army haversack. The ribbon of the Eastern Peoples' Decoration is worn German-fashion in the buttonhole.

D2: First lieutenant, Cossack Cavalry Corps, 1943
Rank is indicated by the shoulder boards, in the sequence prescribed for Russian, Ukrainian and Cossack volunteers. German national insignia are worn on the cap and the breast; otherwise the costume is traditionally Cossack, consisting of the *tcherkesska* and *baschlyk*. He carries the Russian Tokarev M40 semi-automatic rifle and Russian ammunition pouches, as well as the traditional *shashka* sabre.

D3: Kuban Cossack trooper, 1943
The costume is taken from a photo of a unit parading, and is more elaborate than would

(Left): Light-coloured fleece *papashas* were not unusual. This Cossack warrant officer wears regulation collar and shoulder insignia; the transverse rank stripes on the shoulder straps are worn close to the button, in traditional Russian fashion. (Right): Another example of the extraordinary diversity of Cossack volunteer uniforms displayed by a group of Terek Cossacks swearing allegiance on their unit colour.

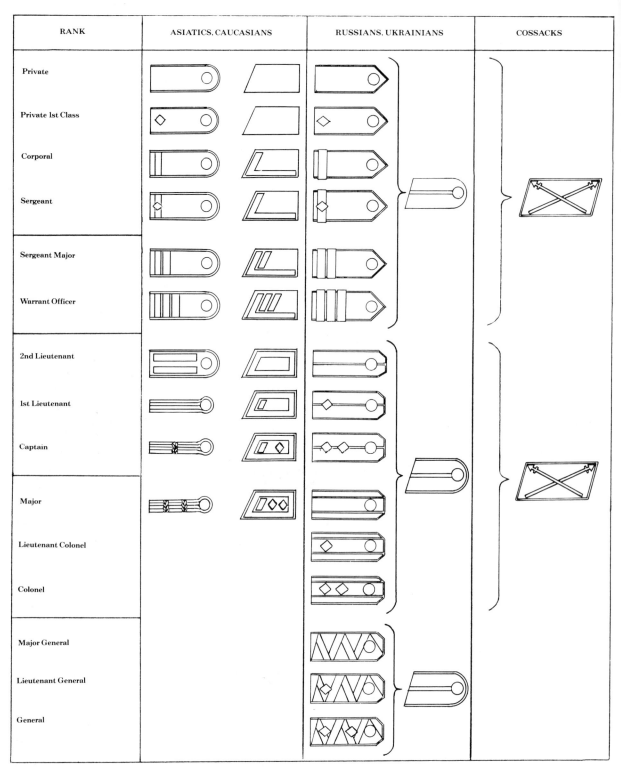

RANK	ASIATICS, CAUCASIANS		RUSSIANS, UKRAINIANS	COSSACKS
Private				
Private 1st Class				
Corporal				
Sergeant				
Sergeant Major				
Warrant Officer				
2nd Lieutenant				
1st Lieutenant				
Captain				
Major				
Lieutenant Colonel				
Colonel				
Major General				
Lieutenant General				
General				

Shoulder straps and collar patches of the Osttruppen:

Asiatic and Caucasian nationalities—**Red collar patches with white braid, bars and 'pips'. Shoulder straps, from private to second lieutenant inclusive, grey ground, red edge piping, white stripes and 'pips'; from first lieutenant to major, narrow silver cords, gold braids for captain and major.**

Russians and Ukrainians—**Black collar patches; privates and NCOs, white stripe, no edge piping; from second lieutenant to colonel,** stripe and edge piping silver; generals, stripe, edge piping and button in gold. Shoulder straps black with red edge piping, all ranks; privates and NCOs, stripes and 'pips' white; second lieutenant to colonel, red stripes and gold 'pips'; generals, gold zig-zag stripes, silver 'pips'.

Cossacks—**Shoulder straps as for Russians and Ukrainians. Red collar patches with white crossed lances; dark green edging for all enlisted ranks, white edging for all officers.**

normally be seen in the front line. The *kubanka* cap has the red top of the Kuban *voiskoi*, with the universal white tape cross. The German M1936 tunic, with Cossack collar patches, bears the Kuban armshield, and is worn under the traditional piped *baschlyk*. The rifle is the standard German Mauser 98k, and is supplemented by a fine *shashka* sabre. The breeches and boots in this case are standard German cavalry issue.

E1: Second lieutenant of an Ostbataillon, 1942–43

From a photo which shows an interesting and typically individual variation on regulations. This Russian junior officer wears the standard German enlisted man's *Feldmütze*, with the white piping 'V' of the infantry enclosing a German cockade, but lacking the German eagle on the crown, and with red piping added all round the turn-up. The collar of the German M1943 field grey tunic has been re-tailored into a 'stand' collar, and this is also piped

Cossacks in German service, in the usual mixture of uniforms and insignia. The officer at left wears the hanging *baschlyk* over a German officer's tunic.

red, and worn without patches. Red piping has been added to standard issue German enlisted man's trousers, tucked into German marching boots. The breast bears the German *Hoheitsabzeichen*, and the shoulders the broad, white-backed silver cord shoulder straps of a German infantry Leutnant. Not one of these features accords with official practice.

E2: Second lieutenant, Terek Cossacks(?), 1944

The *kubanka* has the pale blue top of the Terek *voiskoi*, allowing this tentative identification, but the rest of the uniform gives no clues. The collar patches and shoulder boards of this rank, in the sequence authorised for Russian and Ukrainian troops, are worn on standard German enlisted man's uniform, with Russian boots. A chaotic mixture of different

Unofficial unit cap insignia were known among the Osttruppen; this Caucasian volunteer, wearing a German tunic complete with collar patches and Hoheitsabzeichen, sports a badge in the form of the traditional Circassian *kindjal* dagger on his short-visored mountain troops' field cap.

items from different sequences of insignia, worn promiscuously on German and Russian uniforms, was typical of Osttruppen.

E3: Private, Russian Liberation Army, 1944
Some units serving in the West were issued this blue-grey uniform which in some respects reflects the cut of the traditional Russian *gymnasterka* shirt-tunic. Cloth may have come from old French stocks. Note the breast insignia for non-Germanic volunteers, rarely seen in practice. The other ROA insignia and Soviet equipment are unremarkable.

F1: Senior cavalry NCO, Turkestan Legion, 1943
Standard German cavalry uniform is worn with collar patches and shoulder straps of rank in the sequence authorised for Asiatic and Caucasian

volunteers, and with national armshield and cockade insignia. The armshield is illustrated in detail in an accompanying table; this Legion raised 26 combat battalions.

F2: Major, German artillery, serving with Osttruppen, 1944
Based on photos of an Ostbataillon commander, this figure reminds us that German personnel of branches other than the infantry were often posted to Ostbataillone because of some particular quality or aptitude. The field service uniform of this rank and branch is worn, with the silver-piped *Einheitsfeldmütze* which replaced the officer's sidecap from mid-1943 onward. Red artillery *Waffenfarbe* is seen at collar and shoulder. The ROA armshield is worn, unusually, on the right sleeve. In the tunic buttonhole are a spray of three medal ribbons: the Iron Cross 2nd Class, Eastern Peoples' Decoration for Merit 2nd Class, and Winter 1941/42 Medal. Original photos show, pinned to the left breast the silver sunburst insignia of the Eastern Peoples' Decoration for Merit 1st Class, and German General Assault and black wound badges.

F3: Second lieutenant, Russian Liberation Army, 1944
Junior officer of an Ostbataillon, just awarded the Eastern Peoples' Decoration for Merit 2nd Class; he wears standard German uniform, the tunic and trousers apparently of enlisted man's issue, the cap of officer's type, with silver piping at the crown seam and the front cut-out of the turn-up, and a Russian blue and red cockade. The collar, shoulder and sleeve insignia are conventional.

G1: First lieutenant, Armenian Legion, 1944
German enlisted man's uniform worn with the regulation rank collar patches and narrow shoulder cords of a Zugführer in this Caucasian volunteer legion, which provided some 13 combat battalions for the Wehrmacht. The armshield follows the pattern produced in Germany for Caucasian, Asiatic, and Western European volunteers; exact colours are shown in the accompanying chart.

G2: Warrant officer, Osttruppen, 1945
The combination of the German uniform, the collar and shoulder insignia of the original Asiatic and Caucasian volunteers, and the armshield of the

ROA, reflect the chaotic position which these troops occupied 'on paper'. In practice they had no responsibility towards the ROA, and no loyalty to it.

G3: First lieutenant, Georgian Legion, 1944–45
Interestingly, this Zugführer of one of the 14 combat battalions raised by the Georgian Legion wears German officer's collar and shoulder insignia instead of the regulation pattern as worn by G1. He is believed to have been photographed in Normandy serving with the 795.Ostbataillon. The national armshield is the only special feature on his uniform. The cap is the 'old style officers' field cap', a popular and convenient alternative to the stiff *Schirmmütze* and the *Einheitsfeldmütze*; the tunic is the lightweight summer field pattern, in a greenish shade of field grey.

H1: Unteroffizier, Legion Freies Indien, 1944
This sergeant wears standard German Army tropical uniform, with matching insignia including the copper-brown NCO *Tresse* at collar and shoulder straps; the *Waffenfarbe* is in green, reflecting the redesignation of this unit as a Panzergrenadier regiment. Only the armshield identifies this unit.

H2: Oberleutnant, Legion Freies Indien, 1944
Semi-breeches and long canvas and leather desert

Rare photos of the Deutsch-Arabische Lehr Abteilung in Tunisia, 1943, show a Hauptfeldwebel from Sonderverband 287, in standard German tropical uniform with that organisation's arm insignia; and an Unteroffizier of that unit drilling native recruits, who wear pre-war French Army uniforms without insignia other than the white and black brassard 'Im Dienst der Deutsche Wehrmacht'.(ECPA).

boots were an alternative to the long, loose trousers and ankle boots worn by H1, but not one which depended on rank—theoretically they could be worn by any rank. This officer follows normal DAK practice in retaining the blue/grey-on-tan enlisted man's breast eagle with which his tunic was issued. As a Sikh he wears a turban rather than a field cap.

All items of the uniform are in the varying shades of olive-khaki used for German Army tropical kit.

H3: Private, Legion Freies Arabien, 1943
Apart from the armshield this is the standard DAK infantryman's uniform, with white piping at the shoulder straps.

Notes sur les planches en couleur

A1 Uniforme courant de simple soldat de l'infanterie allemande, ayant pour seules différences l'écusson d'arme en forme de bouclier et l'écusson tricolore sur le casque. Cette forme d'écusson d'arme était courante pour tous les volontaires d'Europe Occidentale et du Caucase et on la trouvait aussi sur certains volontaires originaires des Balkans et de la Baltique. **A2** Un amalgame d'articles d'uniforme français d'avant-guerre et d'articles de l'uniforme des *Afrika Korps*. Les seuls insignes sont l'écusson de cette organisation, qui comprend le motif commun de la hache à double tranchant du régime de Vichy, à droite sur la poitrine; et les galons sur les manchettes. **A3** Uniforme de sous-officier d'infanterie allemande, courant, avec la tresse d'argent montrant le grade portée sur le col et les épaulettes, ainsi que l'écusson d'arme des volontaires wallons sur la manche gauche.

B1 La seule différence sur cet uniforme par rapport à l'uniforme courant de l'officier en service quotidien des forces armées de l'air allemandes est l'insigne la légion croate de l'air, épinglé sur le côté droit de la poitrine sous l'aigle de la *Luftwaffe*. **B2** Cet uniforme est celui du soldat d'infanterie allemande après 1943, avec bottes courtes et guêtres en toile; la tunique a perdu son col vert foncé et les poches ne sont pas plissées. L'écusson national est répété, il s'agit du casque sous une forme simplifiée. **B3** 'Uniforme de débarquement', courant, du *Kriegsmarine* sur lequel l'écusson d'arme croate est ajouté.

C1 Uniforme de campagne des officiers de la *Luftwaffe* à dater de 1943; dans ce cas un écusson national d'arme lettonien des—un des quelques modèles différents. **C2** Les Baltes bénéficiaient d'un statut spécial parmi les *Ostruppen*; ce commandant de bataillon estonien, que l'on peut identifier grâce à son écusson d'arme, porte l'uniforme et l'insigne complets de chef de bataillon de l'infanterie allemande. **C3** Basé sur l'uniforme de général d'armée allemande, avec liseré doré et bandes rouges aux endroits habituels, mais avec l'insigne *ROA* sur la casquette, etles écussons de col et les épaulettes de rang ROA.

D1 Combinaison caractéristique d'éléments d'uniformes russe et allemand. Les écussons appliquées sur le col sont celles spécialement autorisées pour les volontaires cosaques; l'écusson d'arme est en rouge et bleu, couleurs des Cosaques du Don. **D2** Le grade est indiqué par les épaulettes, de la série autorisée pour les volontaires russes, ukrainiens et cosaques. Les insignes allemands sur la coiffure et à gauche sur la poitrine exceptés, le costume est entièrement cosaque. **D3** Uniforme de rassemblement du bataillon, dans une combinaison d'éléments allemands et russes—la *kubanka*, une tunique allemande avec écussons cosaques appliquées sur le col, l'insigne du *Kuban* sur la manche, un *baschlyk*, des bretelles et des bottes de la cavalerie allemande, un fusil allemand et un sabre cosaque.

E1 Un uniforme typiquement original et non autorisé, basé sur la tunique, les pantalons et le calot d'homme de troupe allemand avec liserés ajoutés et retouches de forme. **E2** Un amalgame d'éléments russes et allemands; le haut bleu du *kubanka* fait penser à un officier des Cosaques de la région de Terek, cependant il n'est pas possible de l'identifier avec certitude. **E3** Cet uniforme curieux, probablement créé à partir des stocks de tissu de l'armée française d'avant-guerre, a été distribué à quelques unités russes en Europe Occidentale; son dessin rappelle la traditionnelle *gymnasterka*.

F1 Uniforme courant de la cavalerie allemande, avec écussons de col appliquées, épaulettes, cocarde sur le calot et écusson d'arme autorisé pour les unités asiatiques. **F2** Des officiers d'armes autres que l'infanterie étaient spécialement affectés au commandement des *Ostbataillone* en raison d'expérience ou aptitude spéciales; ce commandant d'artillerie est un exemple. Il n'est pas commun de voir l'écusson d'arme placé sur la manche droite. **F3** Autre uniforme 'inventé' typique destiné à un officier subalterne des volontaires russé et dont la conception est basée sur l'uniforme de l'homme de troupe allemand.

G1 Insigne réglementaire des troupes du Caucase et des troupes asiatiques porté sur un uniforme d'homme de troupe allemand. **G2** L'écusson d'arme *ROA* ajouté aux uniformes des légions originaires du Caucase et des légions asiatiques était une fiction créée par l'administration: les bataillons formés à partir de ces légions n'ont jamais été placés sous le commandement du général Vlasov et étaient en grande partie très hostiles à son organisation.

G3 Des photos intéressantes prises en Italie et montrant cet officier, qui est vraisemblablement de la 162ème 'Turkoman' Division, vêtu de l'uniforme complet d'officier allemand, avec signes distinctifs de grade et d'arme, l'écusson d'arme national excepté. La tunique est un modèle léger d'été.

H1 Uniforme *DAK* courant, écusson d'arme excepté. **H2** Un changement à l'uniforme *DAK*, porté cette fois avec un turban car l'officier est sikh. **H3** Le seul signe distinctif de cette unité en est l'écusson d'arme; sinon l'uniforme tropical courant est porté

Farbtafeln

A1 Standarduniform eines deutschen Infanterie-Gefreiten, abgesehen von dem schildförmigen Armabzeichen und dem Trikolorenzeichen am Helm. Diese Form des Armschilds war bei allen westeuropäischen, kaukasischen und einigen balkanesischen und baltischen Freiwilligen üblich. **A2** Eine Mischung aus Uniformteilen der französischen Vorkriegszeit und des Afrika-Korps. Die einzigen Insignien sind das Vereinsabzeichen mit dem zweischneidigen Beil-Motiv der Vichy-Regierung auf der rechten Brustseite und die Rangstreifen an den Manschetten. **A3** Standarduniform eines Unteroffiziers der deutschen Infanterie, mit silberner Rangtresse an Kragen- und Schulterstreifen und dem Armschild der wallonischen Freiwilligen auf dem linken Ärmel.

B1 Diese Uniform unterscheidet sich von der Bekleidung eines deutschen Luftwaffenoffiziers lediglich durch das Abzeichen der kroatischen Luftwaffenlegion, auf der rechten Brustseite unter dem Luftwaffen-Adler angebracht. **B2** Diese Uniform gehört einem deutschen Infanteristen nach 1943, dazu gehören kurze Stiefel und Gamaschen aus Segeltuch; beim Uniformrock fehlen die dunkelgrünen Kragen- und Schulterstreifen der früheren Modelle, die Taschen sind nicht gefältelt. Der Armschild wird in vereinfachter Form als Helmabzeichen wiederholt. **B3** Übliche 'Landeuniform' für die Kriegsmarine mit zusätzlichem kroatischen Armschild.

C1 Felddienstuniform für Offiziere der Luftwaffe seit 1943; in diesem Fall mit zusätzlichem lettischen Armschild (eines von sieben verschiedenen Mustern). **C2** Die Balten hatten unter den Ostrupen eine besondere Position; dieser estländische Bataillonskommandant, erkenntlich am Armschild, trägt im übrigen die volle Uniform und Ausrüstung eines deutschen Infanteriemajors. **C3** Basierend auf der Uniform eines deutschen Generals, mit goldenen Kordeln und roten Streifen an den üblichen Stellen, aber mit ROA Mützenabzeichen, Kragenspiegel und Schulterstreifen.

D1 Typische Kombination von deutschen und russischen Uniformteilen. Der Kragenspiegel wurde in dieser Form spezielle für Freiwillige der Kosaken freigegeben; der Armschild hat die roten und blauen Farben der Don Kosaken. **D2** Der Rang wird durch die Schulterstreifen angezeigt; die Reihenfolge wurde für russische, ukrainische und Kosaken-Freiwillige freigegeben. Abgesehen von den deutschen Insignien auf der Mütze und der rechten Brustseite ist es eine reine Kosaken-Uniform. **D3** Paradeuniform mit einer Kombination von deutschen und russischen Teilen—der Kubanka, einem deutschen Rock mit Kosaken-Kragenspiegel und Kuban-Ärmelinsignie, einem Baschlyk und deutschen Kavallerie-Kniehosen und -Stiefeln sowie deutschem Gewehr und einem Kosakensäbel.

E1 Eine typische individuelle, nicht authorisierte Uniform, basierend auf Rock, Hosen und Feldmütze eines deutschen Gefreiten, mit zusätzlicher Kordel und einigen Veränderungen. **E2** Eine weitere Kombination von deutschen und russischen Teilen; die blaue Spitze der Kubanka-Mütze verweist auf einen Offizier der Terek Kosaken, aber die Zuordnung ist nicht gesichert. **E3** Diese merkwürdige Uniform wurde vermutlich aus Vorräten von Armeestoffen der französischen Einheiten in Westeuropa; das Design erinnert an die traditionale Gymnasterka.

F1 Übliche deutsche Kavallerieuniform mit Kragenspiegel, Schulterstreifen, Mützenkokarde und Armschild, die für diese asiatischen Einheiten zugelassen waren. **F2** Offiziere von anderen Branchen als der Infanterie wurden wegen ihrer besonderen Erfahrung zum Kommando von Ostbataillonen abgeordnet; dieser Artilleriemajor ist dafür ein Beispiel. Der ROA Armschild auf dem rechten Arm ist ungewöhnlich. **F3** Eine weitere typische 'erfundene' Uniform für einen Junior-Offizier der russischen Freiwilligen, basierend auf einer deutschen Gefreiten-uniform.

G1 Reguläre Insignien für kaukasische und asiatische Truppen auf einer deutschen Gefreitenuniform. **G2** Der ROA Armschild auf den Uniformen der originalen kaukasischen und asiatischen Legionen war eine Fiktion der Armeeverwaltung; die aus diesen Legionen gebildeten Bataillone waren nur namentlich unter General Vlasovs Befehl und standen seiner Organisation feindlich gegenüber. **G3** Interessante Fotos aus Italien zeigen diesen Offizier (vermutlich von der 162. 'Turkoman' Division) mit einer kompletten deutschen Offiziersuniform mit Rang- und Einheitsabzeichen, abgesehen vom nationalen Armschild. Der Rock ist ein leichtes Sommermodell.

H1 Übliche DAK Uniform, abgesehen vom Armschild. **H2** Eine Variation der DAK Uniform, diesmal mit einem Turban getragen, da der Offizier ein Sikh ist. **H3** Nur der Armschild kennzeichnet diese Einheit; im übrigen wird die übliche Tropenuniform getragen.

**DO NOT REMOVE
CARDS FROM POCKET**

**ALLEN COUNTY PUBLIC LIBRARY
FORT WAYNE, INDIANA 46802**

You may return this book to any agency, branch,

or bookmobile of the Allen County Public Library.

DEMCO